Explore Geography

Investigating coasts

Fred Martin

Heinemann

www.heinemann.co.uk/library

Visit our website to find out more information about **Heinemann Library** books.

To order:
☎ Phone 44 (0) 1865 888066
🖹 Send a fax to 44 (0) 1865 314091
💻 Visit the Heinemann Bookshop at www.heinemann.co.uk/library to browse our catalogue and order online.

First published in Great Britain by Heinemann Library, Halley Court, Jordan Hill, Oxford OX2 8EJ, part of Harcourt Education. Heinemann is a registered trademark of Harcourt Education Ltd.

Editorial: Vicki Yates
Design: Dave Poole and Tokay Interactive Limited (www.tokay.co.uk)
Illustrations: Geoff Ward and International Mapping (www.internationalmapping.com)
Picture Research: Hannah Taylor
Production: Duncan Gilbert

Originated by Repro Multi Warna
Printed in China by WKT Company Limited

10 digit ISBN: 0 431 03293 9   (Hardback)
13 digit ISBN: 978 0 431 03293 1 (Hardback)
10 09 08 07 06
10 9 8 7 6 5 4 3 2 1

10 digit ISBN: 0 431 03294 7   (Paperback)
13 digit ISBN: 978 0 431 03294 8 (Paperback)
10 09 08 07 06
10 9 8 7 6 5 4 3 2 1

British Library Cataloguing in Publication Data
Martin, Fred
Investigating coasts
910.9 ' 146
A full catalogue record for this book is available from the British Library.

Acknowledgements
Alamy Images pp. **5**, **7** (Aerofilms), p. **13b** (ImageSelect), p. **19b** (Andre Seale), p. **21** (Paul Thompson Images), p. **25** (Nigel Reed), p. **26** (Alan Curtis), p. **27** (Photofusion Picture Library); Corbis p. **4** (Ric Ergenbright), p. **11b** (Chris North, Cordaiy Photo Library Ltd), p. **20** (Chloe Johnson; Eye Ubiquitous); p. **13t** (Chinch Grynlewicz; Ecoscene), p. **15** (Richard Hamilton Smith), p. **17** (Roger Ressmeyer), p. **23** (Reuters); Empics p. **19t** (PA/ John Giles), p. **22** (John Stillwell); Getty Images p. **8** (Photodisc), p. **10** (Stone), p. **12** (Photodisc), p. **14** (Robert Harding World Imagery), p. **28** (Digital Vision); Reproduced by permission of Ordnance Survey on behalf of The Controller of Her Majesty's Stationery Office, © Crown Copyright 100000230 p. **6**; Rex Features p. **11t** (The Travel Library); Skyscan p. **29** (B Evans).

Cover photograph of beach huts on a beach, reproduced with permission of Getty Images/Digital Vision.

The publishers would like to thank Rebecca Harman, Rachel Bowles, Robyn Hardyman, and Caroline Landon for their help in the preparation of this book.

Every effort has been made to contact copyright holders of any material reproduced in this book. Any omissions will be rectified in subsequent printings if notice is given to the publishers.

Exploring further

Throughout this book you will find links to the Heinemann Explore CD-ROM and website at www.heinemannexplore.com. Follow the links to find out more about the topic.

Contents

Any words appearing in the text in bold, **like this**, are explained in the glossary.

What is a coast?

The **coast** is the name given to the area where the land meets the sea. The edge of the land is called the coastline. Some coastlines are made up of steep **cliffs** with rocky shores. Others have sand or pebble **beaches**, with **sand dunes** and lowland behind them.

The shape of the coastline is always changing. Much of this is because of the movements of **waves** and **currents** in the sea.

See for yourself

1 If you live near the coast, visit it with an adult.

2 Make a sketch of the coastline and label the main features.

3 If you do not live near the coast, find a picture of an area of coastline and draw your sketch from that.

Destroying the land

A steep cliff is a sign that the land is being **eroded**, or worn away, by the sea. The cliff is steep because the sea wears away the rock at the base of it. When this happens the rock above collapses, and so the cliff face moves back.

■ *The white cliffs at Dover in Kent are constantly being eroded by the sea.*

If you look at the coastline on a map you will see that it is not usually straight. It has dips in it called **bays**, and areas sticking out on either side of bays called **headlands**. Bays and headlands are usually made when the soft rock in the bay areas is worn away by the sea more quickly than the hard rock in the headland areas.

Creating new land

New land can be created at the coast. The material for this land can come from the sea or from the land. Beaches are made with material from the sea, such as **sand** and stones and pebbles, called **shingle**.

New land can also be made with material that comes from the land. Rivers wash soil and rock from the land. When they reach the sea, they drop this material. If this is not washed away, it can make new land. This is how a **delta** is formed.

■ *This delta was made with material dropped by the river as it joined the sea.*

The speed of change

Some changes along the coast happen very quickly. Several metres of a cliff can fall into the sea without warning. This happens where the coastline is made from soft clay and sand. Where the rocks of the coastline are hard, change happens much more slowly. It can take thousands of years for the sea to erode hard rocks.

How do we find out what a coast is like?

Maps and photographs

You can find out a lot about a **coast** before you go there by looking at maps and photographs. These will help you to think of questions about it, so that when you are there you can find out some answers. The coastline may have many **bays** and **headlands**, and it may be popular with tourists. You could find out why this is.

Using an atlas

A map in an **atlas** shows you the names of the main headlands and bays around the coastline. A **geological** map shows you the kinds of rock along the coast. You can guess that if the rocks are made of **chalk**, there will be some steep cliffs and **beaches** with **shingle**. Where there are old, hard rocks, such as **granite**, you can guess that there will also be some steep cliffs, but the beaches will be sandy. In some places, rivers flow into the sea through an **estuary**.

Coasts on an Ordnance Survey map

An Ordnance Survey map with a scale of 1:50,000 gives more detail. It shows if the beach is made from sand or shingle, or if it is rocky. **Contours** and **spot heights** show you where there is a cliff. You can use the map **key** to find out about other features. There may also be clues that show how people use the area. A campsite or caravan park may be marked, or there may be a tourist information centre.

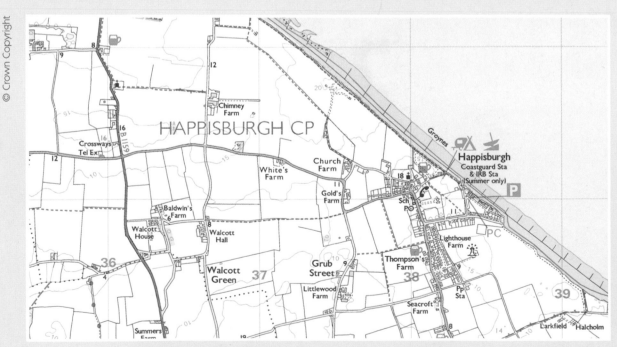

■ *You can use an Ordnance Survey map to find out a lot about a coast. On this map of the east Norfolk coast we can see the area where the caravan park on the opposite page is located.*

Aerial photographs

An **aerial photograph** also shows what the coast is like.

■ It is easy to see a caravan park on an aerial photograph. The caravans are usually set out in rows and they often have white tops to reflect the Sun and keep them cool.

How will we get there and how long will it take?

Nowhere in the UK is more than a few hours' drive from the coast. You can work out how near you are to the nearest stretch of coast by looking at a road map.

How do waves shape coastal environments?

Land along the coastline is gradually eroded by the sea's **waves**. On a calm day, waves lap gently on the **coast**. On a stormy day, they batter the coast with a force that is strong enough to shatter rock. Waves are also one of the ways in which new land is built up along a coast.

■ *The force of the waves can change the shape of the coastline.*

Making waves

Waves are made by the wind. The stronger the wind, the bigger and more powerful the waves become. The biggest waves build up when the wind blows over a long distance of open sea.

The force of the waves

Waves can hit the coast with great force. The weakest rocks are **eroded** fastest. The waves open up any natural cracks in the rocks, until blocks of rock fall down. The sea washes the loose rock away, revealing new rock to be eroded.

Waves pick up loose stones and throw them against the cliffs to wear the rock away even more. Any pieces of rock that the waves break off are taken away by the tide and **currents**. The pieces of rock are washed along the coast, before being dropped in sheltered places, such as **bays**.

You can see how waves move stones and sand along the coast if you watch how waves move on a **beach**. When they are blown by the wind they come up the beach at an angle. They take stones up the beach at the same angle. The water then drains straight back down the beach, also taking stones with it. This moves the stones along the beach in a zigzag. This way that waves and currents move material along the coast is called **longshore drift**.

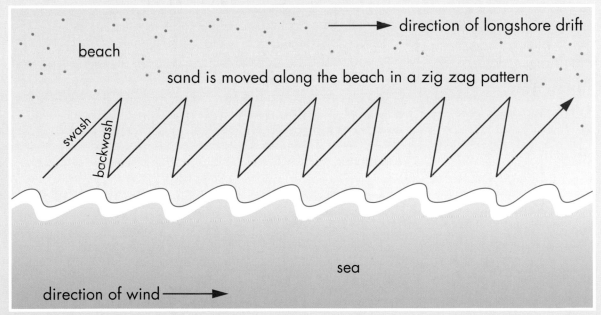

- *This shows the process of longshore drift on a beach.*

Exploring further

On the Heinemann Explore website or CD-ROM go to Exploring > Shaping the coast. Read the article 'Wave attack' to find out more about how waves shape coastal environments. Watch the animation on longshore drift and also try the activity.

Eroding the coast

A coastline has **headlands** sticking out into the sea and **bays** scooped out of the land. **Cliffs** can make spectacular scenery. All these features are formed by **erosion**, sometimes over thousands of years.

Headlands

A headland is a narrow stretch of land pointing out to sea. It is made of rocks that erode more slowly than the rocks around it. A large area of land that points out to sea is called a **peninsula**. The counties of Devon and Cornwall in England are part of a very large peninsula.

■ *Land's End in Cornwall is a headland made from a rock called* **granite***.*

Making a bay

A bay is formed where the sea wears away softer, less **resistant** rocks. There are often headlands at each end of a bay. A **cove** is a narrow bay, with a tiny beach. Coves are often found on rocky coasts.

■ *Durdle Door arch in Dorset is popular with visitors.*

Arches and stacks

An **arch** can form at the end of a headland. The sea wears a hole through the headland, leaving a thin layer of rock across the top. The rock is softer where the hole is made.

A **stack** is a tall pillar of rock that is left standing in the sea. Stacks are formed when an arch collapses. Eventually the stack is also worn away.

■ *A group of stacks called The Needles stand off the west coast of the Isle of Wight. The Needles are made from* **chalk***. They show how the soft chalk coastline is being worn away.*

Sea cliffs

A cliff is where the coastline drops steeply into the sea. Some types of rock, such as chalk, make very steep cliffs. Softer rocks, such as sand or clay, slide into the sea making a more gentle cliff angle.

Cliffs are worn back by the sea. **Waves** cut into them at the bottom and open up cracks in the rock to make **caves**. Part of a cliff can collapse suddenly if there is nothing left at the bottom to support it.

Cliffs made of soft rock can wear back by about 2 metres (6 feet) every year. Several metres can collapse in only a few seconds. Cliffs made of harder rocks, such as granite, are worn back by only a few millimetres every year.

Building up the coast

What is a beach?

Many people's favourite part of a coastline is a **beach**. Beaches can be all shapes and sizes, and can be made from different materials, such as stones, sand, and rock.

Making a beach

The stones and sand on the beach may have been **eroded** from the **cliffs**. **Waves**, **tides** and **currents** move this material along the coast. The eroded material is then dropped in a new place. This is called **deposition**. As this happens, a beach is gradually formed. Some beaches are covered by sand and mud, some are mostly rocky, and some are made from pebbles. Pebbles on a beach are usually called **shingle**.

Where are sand and shingle beaches located?

You can usually tell what type of beach an area will have from the types of rock nearby. A sandy beach will form where the rocks are hard. The sand is made from tiny grains of a mineral such as **quartz**.

If the rock in an area is **chalk**, the beach will probably be shingle of very hard pebbles made of **flint**. This is because there is flint in the layers of chalk. The softer material in the chalk is washed away, leaving the hard flint behind.

■ *People enjoy relaxing on sandy beaches.*

Activity

1. Why do you think people love beaches? Think about the features of your favourite kind of beach.

2. Use an **atlas** to find ten places on the coast of the UK that have a beach. Have you visited any of them?

Beach features

The biggest stones on a beach usually pile up in a ridge at the back, nearest to the land. They are dropped there by the strongest **storm waves**. Waves coming up the beach are strong enough to drop them there, but the water draining back down the beach is not strong enough to drag them back.

▪ *This is a shingle beach made of flint.*

Sometimes, sand and shingle are dropped across the entrance to a bay, or where the coastline changes direction. This makes a narrow ridge of land called a **spit**. A spit can last for hundreds of years, but it is always being attacked by waves and it can be broken during storms.

▪ *Spurn Head is a spit that has grown across the entrance to the River Humber **estuary**, on the north-east coast of England.*

Sand dunes

Low hills of sand behind a **beach** are called **sand dunes**. They have steep slopes and can pile up to a height of about 10 metres (33 feet). The top of a dune is a narrow, sharp, and winding ridge.

Making sand dunes

It takes a lot of sand to make sand dunes. The sand comes from the beach in front of the dunes. The wider the beach, the more sand there is to make the dunes. As the tide goes out, the wet sand dries out. The wind cannot pick up wet sand, but it blows the dry sand up the beach to form dunes.

■ *Sand dunes form when dry sand is blown to the back of a beach.*

Stabilizing the sand

A type of grass called **marram grass** usually grows on sand dunes. The leaves of marram grass are long, narrow and sharp. The roots grow deep into the sand to find water. This helps to stop the sand being blown away.

Many other types of plant grow on sand dunes. The more plants there are in the dunes, the harder it is for the wind to blow the sand away.

■ *Marram grass helps to trap more sand, to make the dunes bigger.*

See for yourself

If you live near a beach with sand dunes, visit them and look closely at the marram grass growing there. You will see that each blade of grass is curled lengthways. Can you think why this might be?

Destabilizing the sand

It is important to make sure that sand dunes do not blow away. This can happen if people destroy the plants on them, or if the wind blows strongly before plants can grow. On some parts of the coast, the sand dunes are all that protect the buildings behind them from the **waves**.

Estuaries and islands

Estuaries

When a river reaches the sea, it can slowly open up to form an **estuary**. The River Severn flows into the Bristol Channel along an estuary. The estuary fills with sea water when the tide is in. When the tide goes out, you can see the river winding its way through the mud along the bottom of the estuary.

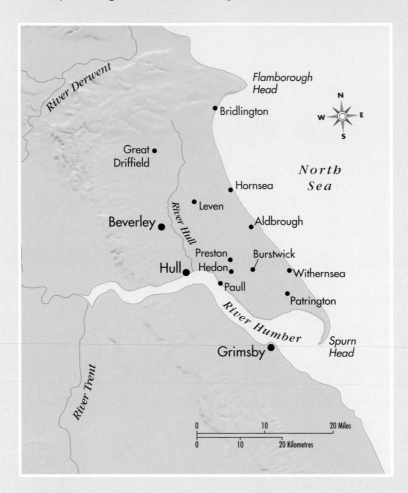

■ The River Humber forms the Humber Estuary as it approaches the sea in the north-east of England. This map also shows the location of Spurn Head Spit, which has formed across the end of the Humber Estuary.

Islands

An **island** is an area of land that is completely surrounded by water. Islands can be any size. England, Scotland, and Wales are all part of one big island called the UK. Some islands are much bigger. Greenland is the biggest island in the world. Some islands are smaller. The Isle of Wight off England's south coast is about 30 kilometres (19 miles) across.

Islands are formed in different ways. Most are made from hard rocks that the sea has not yet **eroded**. Some, such as the island of Hawaii in the Pacific Ocean, are

volcanoes that rise up from the **seabed**.

■ *The island of Hawaii is made up from lava that has erupted from volcanoes.*

Activity

1 Look at a map of the UK, reference books, and the Internet.
2 Find five estuaries in the UK.
3 Name the river that each estuary flows from, and the sea that it meets.
4 Put your information into a table like the one below.

Estuary	The river it flows from	The sea it meets

5 Now name five islands that are off the coast of the UK.
6 Name the country that each island is part of (England, Scotland, Wales, or Northern Ireland).
7 Put your information into a table like the one below.

Island	Country

How does human activity affect coastal environments?

Erosion and deposition

The things that people do along a **coast** affect the coastal landscape. Some activities cause **erosion** and othes cause **deposition**, because everything in the landscape is connected. To understand this, think about where the material that makes a beach has come from. It has usually come from a **cliff**. So if the cliff had not eroded, there would not be a beach.

Cliff protection

People who live near the edge of a cliff usually want the bottom of the cliff to be protected from the **waves**. This will stop the cliff from being eroded and so stop their homes from being lost. Protecting a cliff usually only slows down the rate of erosion. It cannot stop it completely.

If the cliff is protected, however, this will probably affect a beach further down the coast. Sand and other materials are always being moved to and from a beach. If the material is washed away and no more arrives – because the land which produced that material is protected – the beach will gradually disappear.

Cliff collapse

The Holbeck Hall Hotel in Scarborough, in North Yorkshire, was built in 1880 near the edge of a cliff. It was built on soft clay and sand that lay over harder rock. A problem was that rainwater could soak into the upper layer. This made the ground very heavy and unstable. The weight of the hotel added to the problem.

■ In June 1993, the cliff where the Holbeck Hall Hotel stood suddenly collapsed. This is called a **landslide**. Part of the hotel fell into the sea, and the rest of it had to be demolished.

Muddy rivers

Some things that people do far away from the coast can also affect it. For example, when people cut down large numbers of trees, the rain washes away the soil far more quickly than before. This soil gets into rivers, and when they flow into the sea they deposit the mud they have been carrying. This builds up into large **deltas**.

■ The muddy Jucu river in Brazil flows into the Atlantic Ocean.

Holiday coasts

Coastal areas are popular holiday destinations. **Islands** with sandy **beaches** are particularly popular.

Beaches and cliffs

A beach is an ideal place for many kinds of leisure activity, such as swimming, ball games, and sunbathing. A wide, flat, sandy beach is good for children and adults who like building sandcastles and playing family games. **Shingle** beaches are also popular, for example at Brighton and other resorts on England's south coast.

Some people enjoy a walk along the tops of cliffs, as there are beautiful views out to sea. There is a coastal footpath all around the coastline of Devon and Cornwall.

Seaside resorts

Seaside resorts are towns by the sea where people go for a holiday or for a day trip. Many British seaside resorts began to develop about 200 years ago. Blackpool, Bournemouth, Brighton, and other resorts grew quickly.

■ *Piers were built at seaside resorts so that people could walk out over the sea and breathe in the sea air.*

British seaside resorts are still popular, but many people now prefer to go abroad for their main holiday. This is because the British **weather** is not always hot and dry in summer, unlike other places such as Spain, Portugal, and Greece.

Holiday islands

Islands in the Mediterranean Sea are a favourite holiday destination for people in the UK. This is because they can fly there cheaply and quickly. Every year, millions of people from the UK go on holiday to the Spanish Balearic islands of Majorca and Ibiza, the Greek islands of Crete and Corfu, and the Canary Islands of Tenerife and Lanzarote.

Places on these islands that used to be small fishing villages have now become busy seaside resorts. Many hotels, clubs, bars, shops, restaurants, and leisure parks have been built.

■ *Many people like to go on holiday to Majorca. Can you think of the effects this is having on the coastal **landscape**?*

Exploring further

On the Heinemann Explore website or CD-ROM go to Resources > Using coastlines. Watch the video showing the seafront at Brighton to see what a holiday coast looks like.

Working coasts

A **port** is a town or city that is used by passenger or cargo ships. Many of the world's oldest and biggest cities are ports. London, Tokyo, and New York are three of the world's biggest cities that are also ports.

Fishing ports

Peterhead in north-east Scotland and Newlyn in Cornwall are two of the UK's biggest fishing ports. Much of the fishing today is done by a small number of large fishing boats. These boats must follow rules about how many fish they can catch, so that fishing in the future will be **sustainable**.

Ports for trade

A port where big ships bring goods into and out of a country is called a commercial port. **Trade** is the buying and selling of goods. Goods that are **imported** come into a country from outside. Goods that are **exported** go out to another country.

The best place to have a commercial port is where the water is deep, sheltered, and close to the open sea. London, Bristol, and Liverpool are some of the UK's main commercial ports.

■ *Tilbury docks in Essex, to the east of London.*

Activity

1   Look at the labels on some foods at home.

2   Find ten foods that have been imported from another country into the UK.

3   Record the name of the food and where it came from, in a table like the one below.

Food	Country imported from
Cheese	France
Bananas	West Indies

Ferry ports

People drive to a ferry port when they want to take their car or a lorry to another country. For example, ferry boats load up with vehicles at the ferry port at Dover in Kent. The ferry sails to Calais in France, where the vehicles drive off.

Oil ports

Some of the world's biggest ships are oil tankers. They can only use the deepest and biggest harbours. Oil tankers carry large amounts of **crude oil** between countries. The crude oil has to go to an **oil refinery** at an oil port, where it is made into petrol and other fuels.

■ *Sometimes problems occur near oil ports when oil tankers run aground and spill their oil. This causes harm to wildlife and ruins the **beaches** for tourists.*

The Bristol Channel coast

The features of the **coast** are different in different places. Here we will look at a short stretch of the coast along the Bristol Channel, in south-west England.

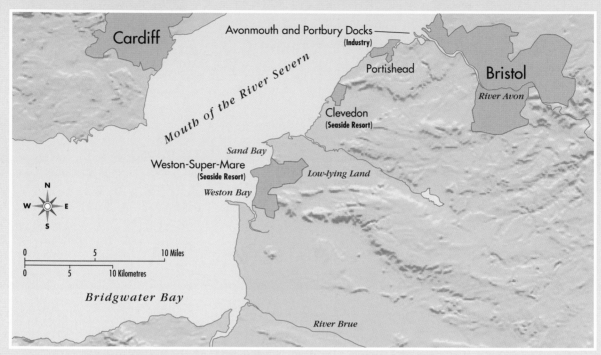

- *The River Severn and the River Avon both flow into the Severn **Estuary**, which then flows into the Bristol Channel. This is a varied coastline, with **headlands** and **bays**. There are also several types of **land use**, including farmland, **seaside resorts** such as Weston-super-Mare, and a big industrial area.*

Rocks and landforms

There are many types of rock in this area. This is one reason why there are both **bays** and **headlands**. Ribs of hard **limestone** run into the sea, with softer bands of clay between them. The headlands form where the limestone is **eroding** slowly. The bays form where the clays are more easily eroded.

Lowlands and floods

The land behind the bays is mostly very low and flat. There used to be a risk of **flooding** by the sea. In most places the land has now been protected so there is little risk of this happening. One problem, however, is that the difference between high tide and low tide in the Bristol Channel is very high, at 14.5 metres (47 feet). This is the second highest in the world. If there is a very high tide at the same time as strong onshore winds, there can still be a risk of flooding.

Coastal land use

There are several types of land use along the coast. Just south of the **mouth** of the River Avon the land is mostly used for industry and docks.

Further south are the towns of Clevedon and Weston-super-Mare, which are both seaside resorts. Clevedon has a **pier,** but it is a quiet resort. Weston-super-Mare is much bigger and busier. It has two piers, theatres, and a wide **beach**.

Between the towns, the land is mostly used for farming. Some farms also have caravan parks where visitors can stay.

■ *Portbury Docks is a huge area. Big container ships come here to **import** and **export** goods.*

Managing coastlines

Why do we need to manage the coastline?

The coastline is always changing. Some of these changes cause problems to people, especially if they happen quickly. This is why people try to manage the coastline.

Walls against the sea

A **sea wall** is one way to manage the coastline. A concrete or rock wall along the seafront helps to stop **waves** from wearing away the land.

■ *Sea walls are usually built at* **seaside resorts** *such as at this one in Scarborough, North Yorkshire.*

It is hard to stop waves from attacking a **cliff**, especially where there is no **beach** in front of it. One way to protect it is by putting piles of boulders at the bottom of the cliff. These break up the force of the waves and so reduce their effect on the cliff.

Low walls called **groynes** are used to stop sand and other beach material from moving along the **coast** by **longshore drift**. A beach helps to protect the land from the waves.

■ *Groynes have been built on many beaches in the UK. They point out to sea in rows, to protect the beach.*

Using nature

Natural features such as **sand dunes** can protect the land from being worn away or **flooded**. The dunes themselves have to be protected so that they are not blown away. One way to do this is to plant grasses and trees on them. The plants make it harder for the wind to blow the sand away.

The powerful sea

All these measures can help to protect the coast, but only for a short while. The sea is too powerful and it will always win in the end. All that we can do is try to slow down its effects.

Exploring further

On the Heinemann Explore website or CD-ROM go to Resources > Using coastlines. This shows you how groynes are used to defend the coast. Think about the beaches you know of where groynes are used to protect the beach.

How will a proposed development affect the coastal environment?

People want to use and develop the coastline around the UK in many different ways. Some want to use it to build accommodation for holidays others want to use it for industry such as **oil refining**. The coastline is also one of the most attractive parts of the country, with rare plants and wildlife, especially birds. It seems a shame to allow building in places such as these.

■ *Do you think that building this power station has spoiled the coastal environment?*

Building a hotel

A new hotel will affect the coastal environment in several ways. A new building can look attractive if it is designed carefully, but can also ruin the natural appearance of the **landscape**. A road will have to be built to take people to the hotel, and there will have to be pipes and cables for water, **sewage**, electricity, and gas, though most of these could be under the ground.

A hotel will also bring more people to the area. People create noise and **pollution**.

- *How do you think the local area was affected when this hotel was built?*

Who is affected?

Several kinds of people will be affected by a new hotel. It will bring jobs to local people. It will attract more visitors, so there will be more customers in the local shops. The people who come on holiday will lead to jobs being created in the area, but also to more traffic.

Local people may like their **beach** because it is quiet, so they will not be happy about more people coming to the area. People who are interested in nature will not want the wildlife to be disturbed.

Activity

Imagine that you live in a coastal area and a new hotel is going to be built near your home. Write a letter to the local council, explaining how you feel about it and the effects it will have on the area.

Making a decision

The **council** has to give permission before anything can be built. People can write to the council or talk to their local councillor to make their views known. If people do not like what their councillors do, they can vote for someone different at the next local election. Councillors need to remember this when they make decisions.

Another way to make a decision is to hold a planning enquiry. At an enquiry a planning inspector listens to all the evidence on both sides, then writes a report to say what he or she thinks about the plan. A government politician makes the final decision. **29**

Glossary

aerial photograph   picture taken from the air

arch   coastal landform where erosion has worn a hole through a headland

atlas   book of maps

bay   landform created where the sea has worn away softer, less resistant rocks

beach   landform made from sand and stones that have been dropped along a coastline

cave   small opening in a cliff

chalk   type of rock

cliff   steep wall of rock next to the sea

coast   area where the land meets the sea

contours   lines on a map that join points of equal height

council   the local government organisation that makes plans for the local area

cove   type of bay that is almost completely surrounded by land, with only a narrow entrance to the sea

crude oil   oil in its natural state

current   strong surge of water that flows constantly in one direction in the sea

delta   muddy pile of sediment formed when a river meets the sea. It looks like a giant fan from the air.

deposition   when a river or the sea drops its load

erosion   wearing away of rocks and soil by wind, water, or ice

estuary   place where a river widens out as it enters the sea

exports   goods that go out to another country.

flint   very hard kind of rock

flooding   when the land is covered by water

geology   the study of rocks

granite   very hard kind of rock

groyne   low wall used to stop sand and other beach material from moving along the coast by longshore drift

headland   cliff sticking out into the sea at the end of a bay

imports   goods that come into a country

island   area of land that is completely surrounded by water

key   panel to explain the features on a map or graph

landscape   the scenery and its features

landslide   sudden movement of material down a slope

land use   how people use the land

limestone   kind of rock made from calcium carbonate

longshore drift   how waves and currents move material along the coast

marram grass   type of grass that usually grows on sand dunes

mouth   end of a river, where it flows into the sea

oil refinery   factory where crude oil can be made into petrol and other fuels

peninsula   land with water on three sides

pier   walkway extending out into the sea

pollution   dirt in the air or water

port   place on the coast or on a large river where ships load and unload their cargo

quartz   hard type of rock found in rocks and sand

resistant   hard to wear away

sand   tiny pieces of rock that are dropped together, usually on a beach

sand dune   hill of sand behind a beach

sea wall   concrete or rock wall along the seafront

seabed   bottom of the sea

seaside resort   town where people go for a seaside holiday or a day trip

sewage   waste material carried away in drains

shingle   small stones on a beach

spit   landform created when sand and shingle are dropped across the entrance to a bay, making a narrow ridge of land

spot height   height of a place marked on a map

stack   tall pillar of rock in the sea

storm wave   large wave that only occurs during a storm

sustainable   able to carry on into the future

tide   the movement of the sea toward the land and away from the land

trade   buying and selling goods

volcano   mountain that erupts molten rock called lava

wave   ripple in the surface of the sea caused by the wind

weather   the condition of the atmosphere at one point in time, which can change every day

Find out more

Books

Mapping the UK: Mapping coasts, Louise Spilsbury (Heinemann Library, 2005)

Landscapes and people: Earth's changing coasts, Neil Morris (Raintree, 2004)

Websites

www.bbc.co.uk/schools/riversandcoasts/mainmenu.shtml
Learn all about coasts (and rivers). Watch the animations to see how particular features are formed.

www.heinemannexplore.com
You will be able to discover much more about coasts by visiting the water section of the Heinemann Explore Website. You can see videos and animations, as well as trying out activities and looking at lots of photographs.

Index

Titles in the *Explore Geography* series include:

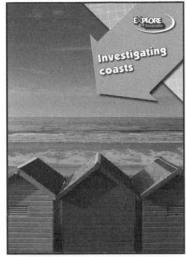

Hardback   0 431 03293 9

Hardback   0 431 03254 8

Hardback   0 431 03257 2

Hardback   0 431 03252 1

Hardback   0 431 03251 3

Hardback   0 431 03253 X

Hardback   0 431 03256 4

Hardback   0 431 03255 6

Find out about other titles from Heinemann Library on our website www.heinemann.co.uk/library